a pocketful of

RHYME

Imagination for a new generation

2006 Poetry Competition for 7-11 year-olds

Young**Writers**

Surrey Vol II
Edited by Heather Killingray

 Young**Writers**

First published in Great Britain in 2006 by:
Young Writers
Remus House
Coltsfoot Drive
Peterborough
PE2 9JX
Telephone: 01733 890066
Website: www.youngwriters.co.uk

SB ISBN 1 84602 604 0

Foreword

Young Writers was established in 1991 and has been passionately devoted to the promotion of reading and writing in children and young adults ever since. The quest continues today. Young Writers remains as committed to the nurturing of poetic and literary talent as ever.

This year's Young Writers competition has proven as vibrant and dynamic as ever and we are delighted to present a showcase of the best poetry from across the UK and in some cases overseas. Each poem has been selected from a wealth of *A Pocketful Of Rhyme* entries before ultimately being published in this, our fourteenth primary school poetry series.

Once again, we have been supremely impressed by the overall quality of the entries we have received. The imagination, energy and creativity which has gone into each young writer's entry made choosing the poems a challenging and often difficult but ultimately hugely rewarding task - the general high standard of the work submitted ensured this opportunity to bring their poetry to a larger appreciative audience.

We sincerely hope you are pleased with this final collection and that you will enjoy *A Pocketful Of Rhyme Surrey Vol II* for many years to come.

Contents

Aimee Hill (11)   111
Ashley Walker (11)   112
Abigail Church (11)   113
Connie Howard (9)   114
Charlotte Worcester (11)   115
Tom Critchley (9)   116
Danny Booth (11)   117
Liam Field   118
Joshua Bell (11)   119
Oliver Newport (11)   120
Seanne Kohler (11)   121
Harry O'Leary (11)   122
Elizabeth Williams (11)   123
Isobel Ruffle (10)   124
Thomas Mulligan (11)   125

St Thomas of Canterbury School, Guildford
Katherine Gilbert (11)   126
Toby Eden (10)   127
Dominic Male (11)   128
Lawrence Bird (11)   129
Emma Sewell (11)   130
Vicky Maguire (11)   131
Dylan Bonds (11)   132
William Gifford McGuiness (11)   133
Bethany Newman (11)   134
Daniel Price (11)   135
Jade Coombes (10)   136
Hannah Gibbs (11)   137
Grace Phelan (11)   138
Christopher Boyle (11)   139
Alex Lillistone (10)   140
Harri Jones (11)   141
Julien Amoruso (10)   142
Philippa Juliff (11)   143
Lily Burtness (10)   144
Stuart Gray (11)   145
Michael Thornton (11)   146

The Russell School

The Poems

Come On England!

There's the kick-off whistle,
With England in the World Cup Final,
England are just playing the ball around,
Hoping they can open up the goals,
David Beckham running down the wing,
He plays it into the box,
Where many players are waiting,
The ball goes high, straight to Owen,
Can he make something of this cross?
The ball falls to his head,
Past the goalie,
And into the net,
Yes! Come on England,
One-nil to England.
The opposition take their kick-off,
And the game has restarted,
That's it, half-time has come,
Beep! The game is up and running again,
It's very quiet, nothing's happening,
England are very tense to keep their lead,
We're in the last 15 minutes,
10 minutes,
5 minutes,
England can't wait for the whistle,
Beep! Beep! Beep!
'Yes, come on England.'
We've won the FIFA World Cup 2006,
Come on England!

Connor Maltby (11)
Beaufort Primary School

A Caterpillar's Day

Caterpillars are crawling up a tree
And then they turn and what do they see
Tumbling down a rocky old hill
Eating a banana about to be peeling,
Pouncing around pretending to be king?
Lions roaring and animals jumping,
Loud and annoying.
There are little old hyenas
And now the day has nearly ended
Soon to be a butterfly.

Rebecca Ly (11)
Beaufort Primary School

My Mad Pet!

My pet is as mad as a monkey,
He is very, very weird,
His fur is as brown as creamy chocolate,
But he is starting to grow a beard!

My pet is as cute as a cuddly cat,
He can run as fast as light,
He can be very lively,
So lively, he doesn't sleep at night.

Can you guess my pet?
I like him so, I give him a snog,
Can you guess my pet?
You guessed it . . . *It's a dog!*

Ceri Anne Green (10)
Beaufort Primary School

Canada

Canada is an enormous place
Where people walk at their own pace.
Niagara Falls, a wonder of the world
And the CN Tower that stands high above the crowd.

In winter it gets very cold
When lots of hats, gloves and scarves are sold.
There's lots of ice and lots of snow
Making lots of fun places for kids to go.

In the summer it gets very warm
Which sometimes creates a very big storm.
When I went to Canada there were lots of things to do
So next time I hope you can come too.

Liam Brabrook (10)
Beaufort Primary School

Animals And Games

Birds can fly,
Cats are happy,
Dogs are sad,
Chicks are hungry,
Games are cool,
Crash is a fox,
Football is funny,
Madagascar is cool.

Andrew Widdicombe (10)
Beaufort Primary School

The Queen

The Queen is here,
Her birthday's near.
The royal gathering here to see,
The one and only.

They walk by the riverside
To see her with pride,
Going on the red carpet in her ride.

And when you see the Queen's cake
You only want to take,
But before you take, you give.
For royal you see
You want to be.

For the Queen supports England
And watches them on TV.
Hopefully she will be happy
And shout yippee!

Jake Dorey (11)
Beaufort Primary School

Old Man

There once was an old man
driving around in his white van.
He drives his van very fast,
he went so fast he went back to the past.
He jumped out his van and spun around,
and after a while he fell to the ground.
He got up and went into his van,
then something hit his window, it looked like a frying pan.
He tried to fix his window,
then came a flamingo and it came and pecked his window.
He asked a man to come and fix it
but all he wanted to do was eat a biscuit.

Paul Dawson (11)
Beaufort Primary School

Deep Blue Sea!

In the deep blue sea,
Where the fish like to play,
There was a big blue shark,
Eating fish every day.

Chomp, chomp, chomp,
Munch, munch, munch,
Yum, yum, yum
Fish in my tum!

Sob, sob, sob,
Went all the other fish,
That big shark
Is eating our children in his dish!

Chomp, chomp, chomp,
Munch, munch, munch,
Yum, yum, yum,
Fish in my tum!

Emel Augustin (10)
Beaufort Primary School

Teams

Man U are red,
Chelsea are blue,
All the rest are green and pink,
That's all I have to say to you.

Rooney is the best,
He's better than all the rest.
If he should score,
The crowd will roar
And all I can say is yay.

Thamed Hussain (11)
Beaufort Primary School

Paula Radcliffe

Aching arms,
Tired legs,
Sweaty feet
As she runs in the heat.

Training hard all day long,
To get this far
She can't go wrong.

The klaxon goes,
The race begins.
There are people ahead
But she will win!

Stephanie Withers (11)
Beaufort Primary School

Football Fun!

F ootball is fun, I always go to soccer camp which is

O pen in the summer. All

O f my friends are there, there are lots of balls flying

T hrough the air, I take my penalty,

B ut the ball

A lways misses.

L ater on there are lots of matches and when I say

L ots I mean lots.

F ree time is after lunch, this is when you can do whatever you
                                                            want, then

U sually you would go to more matches, then it is time for home,

N o I don't want to go home, but my mum says you always have
     tomorrow or next week.

Liam Varndell (11)
Beaufort Primary School

My Pet Giraffe

I've got this pet giraffe,
He lives in our shed,
His head sticks out the roof
And I can see him from my bed.
You can't see his hooves or his tail,
I take him out for walks -
He has a long lead.
Now you've heard about my daft giraffe,
Maybe you would like to see him.

Daniela Roberts (9)
Beaufort Primary School

A Fluffy Tail

A fluffy tail swaying in the night,
A fluffy tail swaying like a rope,
A fluffy tail hanging like a vine in a big oak tree,
A fluffy tail curling around a branch.
The fluffy tail belongs to a kitten
Clinging on tight to a hovering broomstick.

Kieran Bruce (8)
Beaufort Primary School

My Whiny Brother Ryan

My brother Ryan,
Always acts like a lion.
Has a fuss about everything,
Can't even sing!
Is very good at reading,
But not at leading.
Eats hardly anything,
Nowhere near as much as a king.
That's the end of my story,
Not really full of glory.

Niall Anderson (9)
Beaufort Primary School

Oh The Queen, The Wonderful Queen

Oh the Queen, the glorious Queen,
How wonderful she can be.
She walks around
Without a frown,
Oh the faithful Queen.

She is so victorious,
Happy and glorious,
So active and powerful,
Also so loyal
Because she is a great Royal.

Sakinah Abdullah (9)
Beaufort Primary School

Ray Mysterio

Ray Mysterio here we go,
From the top ropes to the floor below.
Here we go.
From the ring he is the champ,
From his mean body slam,
Heavily he kicks the ramp.

Adam Richards (9)
Beaufort Primary School

Hot Chocolate

Mixing and mixing the chocolate and the water
Waiting for it to be ready.
The warmth trickling down your throat,
Tasting the chocolate bits.

Swirling around in your cup,
The taste of a milky hot snack,
Drinking it really fast
With gasp of amazement.

Staring at your friend drinking theirs,
Then you'll beg for another one!

Ryan Ly (9)
Beaufort Primary School

My Weird And Wonderful Pets

You would not believe how many weird pets I have!

I have a big blue dog with a big bald belly,
And a pink and purple warthog with a tail made of jelly.

A little tiny elephant with ears as big as Mars,
And a huge green monkey who plays with real cars.

A silver robotic cat with multicoloured flashing ears,
And a little turquoise bunny who chases orange deer.

A yellow kangaroo with a rather silly bounce,
Who has a big, huge joey who can really, really pounce.

Why I have these animals I'm really not so sure,
'Cause all of that was a bag of lies, I hope I don't tell more.

Jiordan Webb-Mundy (9)
Beaufort Primary School

Kitten And Cat

Cute kitten runs along the path,
Runs so fast, runs so quick,
Meets a cat so beautiful,
Heart begins to beat.

Cat looks at kitten,
Her heart starts to beat,
Kitten then looks at cat,
They ran to each other and purr.

Reece Evans (10)
Beaufort Primary School

My Mum Won't Let Me!

My mum won't let me go to sleepovers or tea parties,
She won't even buy me a pet,
I think it's because it will mess everywhere.
She won't let me do cooking or horseriding,
She won't let me go to fighting clubs,
If I do I will beat my brother forever.
She won't let me go anywhere,
It's just not fair!

Hinna Ghafoor (9)
Beaufort Primary School

Florida

I got on the plane,
Feeling quite insane,
I was going to the home of sunshine.

Yes! I was in the fabulous USA,
I knew I would have a marvellous day,
Now I was in the fantastic Florida.

I went to Disney, Seaworld, Universal too,
The place is as perfect as Heaven, it's true,
It really was a holiday of a lifetime.

There was white sand like diamonds,
The clear sea swishing on the sand that bonds,
Like a princess beach from a fairytale.

It was sad to go,
From the place I got to know,
And I loved everything.

From the hot fudge sundaes to the parks,
Everything makes sparks,
As it's all as lovely as a dream.

My nan made that dream come true,
And showed me things all new,
I love her very much for everything she does.

Natalie Maher (10)
Beaufort Primary School

The Field

Behind my house is a field,
The birds swoop high in the sky,
The butterfly flutters from plant to plant,
Ants scurry under my feet,
Boys playing football and having great fun,
A pony whinnies and stamps her foot,
I can see a blackbird making a nest,
I can smell the sweet fragrance of the foxglove,
The wind blows and rustles my hair,
I see a deer, its ears show over the tips of grass,
This is the field, the field behind my house.

Robyn Evans (11)
Beaufort Primary School

The Big Celebrations

As the Queen walks by with her big, shiny crown,
The Royal Family clapping,
The Queen's choir singing when England win the World Cup,
The Queen sings along with the England squad.
When the Queen's riding across the red carpet on her gold chariot,
With everybody singing and chanting,
The loud music and the swaying makes the Queen happy.
When all the people come home and turn on the TV
And listen to the Queen's speech,
That's why all the people admire the Queen.

Charlie Youens-Allen (11)
Beaufort Primary School

The World Cup

T alented players
H onour and pride
E uropean fans

W orst players to best
O ldest players
R est of the best players
L owest scores at times
D own-hearted players

C ountries play for their people
U nited they get the World Cup
P lay the best players

Come on England!

Matthew Stevens (10)
Beaufort Primary School

The Jungle

Towering trees above my head,
Sunlight creeping through the gaps of the leaves,
Scorpions scuttling across the jungle floor,
I wish I could stay here forever.
Monkeys and apes,
Swinging in trees,
Insects and flies,
Buzzing around my head and knees.
The blazing sun,
Burning my head,
Sweaty feet,
Now I'd rather be in bed!
Chirping noises from the birds above,
Chimpanzees padding across the jungle floor,
Dead leaves lying helplessly in heaps,
I need to get home quick!
I'm in a state, flapping and panicking,
I'm all by myself trekking through the jungle,
I need to find an exit from this place,
Please somebody . . . *help!*

Lucy Colleer (11)
Beaufort Primary School

Mighty Dragons

Dragons ruled the sky with their great powers.
Then they started ruling jewelled towers.
Dragons shock you on first sight.
No one can defeat them, not even a knight.
Dragons can shoot balls of fire.
Each day they fly even higher.
Dragons started ruling the sea.
Now every sailor is going to flee.
Dragons now have to go
But how do we really know?

Leayah Smith (11)
Beaufort Primary School

Housework

Housework is something you have to do
Keep it tidy, instead of it looking like a zoo
Housework may seem boring
But some people might find it enjoying
All the washing, ironing and hovering may seem like no fun
But someone has to get it all finished, done
There may be better things to do
Than cleaning the loo
You would rather be playing cricket or football
Instead of dusting the top corners of the wall
Then when you've done it *all*
You can get back to playing football!

Jason Foskett (10)
Beaufort Primary School

Dolphins

Dolphins are cute,
Dolphins are bright,
Dolphins can swim left and right.

Dolphins are cuddly,
Dolphins are soft,
Dolphins are lovely.

Dolphins are sweet,
Dolphins are cute,
Dolphins are fantastic.

Dolphins are good friends,
Dolphins can jump,
Dolphins are the best *'ever'!*

Dolphins are pretty,
Dolphins are happy,
Dolphins are incredible.

Dolphins are great,
Dolphins are cheeky,
Dolphins are chatty.

Dolphins squeak,
Dolphins are warm,
Dolphins are cute.

Dolphins are soft,
Dolphins are beautiful,
Dolphins are smooth.

Dolphins are strong,
Dolphins are not strong,
Dolphins are super-duper.

Dolphins are excellent,
Dolphins are the best at jumping,
Dolphins are prettier then *'ever'!*

Misbah Hussain (10)
Beaufort Primary School

Hate

Black is the colour of hate, like the dull dark sky.
It sounds like the cracking wall of death.
It tastes sour like gone off milk.
It smells like the horrid smell of rotten eggs.
It looks like two dogs fighting over a bone.
It feels like someone punching me on a pavement.
It reminds me of people breaking up.

Megan Bolton (9)
Beacon Hill Community Primary School

Fun

Fun is a burst of colours like a rainbow shimmering
in the highest sky,
It sounds like the tinkling of a merry-go-round at the busy fair,
It tastes like the sweetness of sugary marshmallows
dissolving in your mouth,
It smells like the scent of a strong rose,
It looks like the brightness of balloons floating past the clouds,
It feels like rain splashing on your head,
It reminds me of the funniest joke in the world.

Amelia Bocutt (9)
Beacon Hill Community Primary School

Loneliness

Loneliness is grey, like there is no colour in the world,
It sounds like rain dripping on the ground,
It tastes like a cold bowl of porridge waiting to be eaten,
It smells like dead flowers in a vase,
It looks like cold air flowing around an old tree,
It feels like a dusty old box in a corner,
It reminds me of a book in the loft.

Milly Claxton (9)
Beacon Hill Community Primary School

Darkness

Darkness is black like an endless gloomy hole
It sounds like a thundering sky above my head
It tastes like a cold bowl of rotten stew sitting in front of me
It smells like the bitter scent of oranges sitting in the bin
It looks like a dusty grey mist covering up the bright horizon
It feels like the coldness of a dreadful frosty January night
It reminds me of a murky, grubby, stormy cloud following me
                                                    wherever I go.

Emilia Chubb (9)
Beacon Hill Community Primary School

Sadness

Sadness is as pale as someone who is ill.
It sounds like the wind howling and rustling through the trees.
It tastes like salty water swimming out of your eyes
                                          and into your mouth.
It smells like an onion that makes you cry.
It looks like someone being sent to bed on Christmas Day.
It feels like a deserted house in a mournful forest.
It reminds me of when Manchester United lost the FA Cup.

Adam Bryant (9)
Beacon Hill Community Primary School

The Magic Box

(Based on 'Magic Box' by Kit Wright)

I will put in my magic box a . . .

Powerful panda that prances proudly,
A piece of steel from the strongest steel of all.
One leaping lion that has launched off a large lollipop.

I will put in my magic box a . . .

A human in the stable.
A surfer in a pool.
A pony ice skating.
A swimmer in the middle of the sea.

I will put in my magic box . . .

Carbon dioxide that is the colour of the rainbow.
There's red air in my box from a dragon's breath.
Indigo petals that fell from the flowers.

My magic box . . .

Is made from carbon dioxide
And mythical phoenix blood.
The hinges are made from liohorkide
There are secrets stuffed in the lid,
There are wishes in the corners.

I will sit in my small box and shut the lid.
(It has a lot of space).
I will play all night.

Louise Bowers (9)
Beacon Hill Community Primary School

The Magic Box

(Based on 'Magic Box' by Kit Wright)

I will put in my box . . .
A robber that's rough, roaring and ruthless,
Boots that are brewing beefy broth.

I will put in my box . . .
A sheep crossed with a hog, and a ten-legged snake
With a flying clock and a bird that tells the time.

I will put in my box . . .
Golden care, lilac odour and smelly green happiness
Blowing blue musical chewing gum
In triangular big bubbles.

My box will be made of
Dogs' noses for the corners
Elephants' skin for the box's outer lining
And the filling full of rabbits' tails.

Alexander Jones (9)
Beacon Hill Community Primary School

The Magic Box

(Based on 'Magic Box' by Kit Wright)

I will put in my box . . .

A cute careful cat
that wears a crimson cardigan
and that goes crazy at Christmas.

I will put in my box . . .

A pink moon and a talking flower
A barking cat, a miaowing dog.

I will put in my box . . .

A black smell and blue gas twirling around in the air
And green gravity that spins me around.

On my box the lid is made from . . .
A witch's cape.
The hinges are made from . . .
A dragon's teeth.
The sides are made of . . .
A shining sun with a shadow.

Keren Howard (8)
Beacon Hill Community Primary School

Fun

Fun is bright orange just like the beaming sun,
It sounds like a bird singing at the crack of dawn,
It tastes like a sour, bitter lemon squeezed on your pancakes,
It smells like sweet pollen from a bright red rose,
It looks like a daisy about to bloom,
It feels like a soft feather floating down from the sky,
It reminds me of golden sand on the beach in the summer holidays.

Ione Fox (9)
Beacon Hill Community Primary School

The Magic Box

(Based on 'Magic Box' by Kit Wright)

I will put in my box . . .
A slithery snake, sliding slowly
Along a hundred chocolate cup cakes.

I will put in my box . . .
Dogs speaking and people barking
Raining wooden drops and trees made of water.

I will put in my box . . .
A red sky and a blue sun
Emerald wishes from my best friend

My box is made from the hair of a dragon,
The hinges are made from the bones of a T-Rex
And the lid is made from horses' hooves and pigs' ears.

Ryan Dennis (9)
Beacon Hill Community Primary School

Silence

Silence is white like a small lonely room in a planet of quietness,
It sounds like a world where nobody exists,
It tastes like the stale air in an old cellar,
It smells like someone's abandoned dinner on the table,
It looks like a black and white film in the cinema,
It feels like sand trickling through your fingers,
It reminds me of the noiseless universe.

Teagan Marshall (9)
Beacon Hill Community Primary School

The Magic Box

(Based on 'Magic Box' by Kit Wright)

I will put in my box . . .

A slow swish of a swaying star through a winter's night,
Cold air from the freezing North Pole,
The food from a farming farmer in the south.

I will put in my box . . .

The 13th month of the year and a red moon,
A creepy castle in the middle of a village,
A brick church in the middle of the ocean.

I will put in my box . . .

Two black words from an ant,
One white miaow from the dog,
Ten purple words spelt from the dust.

My box is made of the finest rain,
With silver splinters for my hinges
And all the secrets in the box to save them from evil.

Rachael Lawrence (9)
Beacon Hill Community Primary School

The Magic Box

(Based on 'Magic Box' by Kit Wright)

I will put in the box . . .

A catapulting camel from a crazy civilisation
A fiery, frustrating football fan, throwing a fight
A hairy, hopping, hollow head

I will put in my box . . .

A 13th month of the season
A snorting bird
A singing pig

I will put in my box . . .

A blaze of red from a deep voice
A skim of blue from the long sky
A shine of yellow from the blinding sun

It's as big as a blue whale
As glamorous as a pop star
And as shiny as a diamond.

Calum Ridgewell (9)
Beacon Hill Community Primary School

Sadness

Sadness is grey like fading flowers in a dark corner,
It sounds like a heart-stopping cry from a graveyard,
It tastes like the damp sponges drying up,
It smells like the strongest scent that could make you cry,
It looks like people in hospital dying,
It feels like the harsh bullies going at me,
It reminds me of boiling water burning me.

Prina Patel (9)
Beacon Hill Community Primary School

Love

Love in pink like a bright open rose closing at the end of summer,
It sounds like soft music developing into a gentle bed of notes,
It tastes like candy and chocolate,
Smothering your mouth with sweetness,
It smells like blossom in the middle of spring,
It looks like the sun raining down on the swimming pool
And looks full of glitter,
It feels like a huge great hug from your duvet,
It reminds me of a married couple walking down the alleyway.

Sophie Stokes (9)
Beacon Hill Community Primary School

Loneliness

Loneliness is grey, grey like an empty room.
It sounds like the distant chatter of people.
It tastes like a bowl of uncooked rice.
It smells like Brussels sprouts, steaming in a hot metal pan.
It looks like an empty and deserted house.
It feels like a grey thundercloud storming in my palm.
It reminds me of driving along a blank and unknown road.

Laura Wyeth (9)
Beacon Hill Community Primary School

My Friend Keren

K ind and fun.

E nergetic.

R eally good friend.

E ager to learn.

N ever mean.

Atessa Tafreshi (8)
Beacon Hill Community Primary School

Hallowe'en

H owling werewolves
A scary night
L aughing and roaring from monsters
L anterns glowing in the dark
O ld ghosts roaming the streets
W itches stirring up spells
E vil skeletons haunting the houses
E ndless thunderstorms all night
N eighbour's shrieks pass in the wind.

Charlotte Swadling (9)
Beacon Hill Community Primary School

The Magic Box

(Based on 'Magic Box' by Kit Wright)

I will put in the box . . .
Chips to chomp on
Covered in ketchup
And tasting yummy.

I will put in the box . . .
A pig climbing a tree.
A monkey going oink.

I will put in the box . . .
A frog going *snap, snap*
And a crocodile going *croak.*

I will put in the box . . .
A silver cat sleeping
With a gloomy ghost having nightmares.

My box is made of . . .
Bright gold and black diamonds
With a red, red crown.

Charley Barker (9)
Beacon Hill Community Primary School

I Wish, I Wish

I wish, I wish
I were a fish
In May I swam all day
I licked a dish
And it smelt delicious
And ate no more today.

Sophie Messiha (8)
Holy Cross Preparatory School

Space

Space from Earth is a dark space,
Along the stars, it's a very bright sight,
But it's mostly nice at *midnight!*
When they all come out from a great height!

Camille Wouters (7)
Holy Cross Preparatory School

Dogs

I wish dogs could make a wish
A wish that would make a dish
A dish with a fish that could wish.

But oh no! Here comes a cat
What shall I do?
I know that cats eat fish
But what shall I do?
I know what to do.
I'll wish that cats can wish for a kitten,
But not any kitten, a kitten for a cat.

Oh no, a bird, what shall I do?
I know what to do.
I'll make a good wish.
I wish that everyone is back to normal!
It's fine now.

Emilia Skeates (8)
Holy Cross Preparatory School

Poems

Poems big, poems small,
Poems hanging on the wall.
Poems about cats, dogs and fish.
Pirates falling down the loo!
Giraffes running races with goals made of jelly!
Girls with baskets, full of fruit and bread.
Boys with top hats.
All these things are contained in a poem.
I love poems.

Georgia Kirby (7)
Holy Cross Preparatory School

Little, Little Children

Little, little children, where have you gone?
On the climbing frame or exploring the Milky Way.
Little, little children, where have you gone?
Did you go with your friends or straightening your hair?
Little, little children sleeping on the hay,
Dreaming nice dreams all, all day.

Sowmiya Murukathash (8)
Holy Cross Preparatory School

Fairies, Fairies

Fairies, fairies, where are you?
In the garden or down the loo.
Fairies, fairies, I've found you, I'll have some fun
Let's play with everyone
Fairies, fairies, time will fly
Now go and say goodbye.

Claire Rich (8)
Holy Cross Preparatory School

Animal Alphabet

A is for ants who like to crawl into people's pants!

B is for bears, big and growly, so please don't break their chairs.

C is for crabs, don't poke them or else they'll grab!

D is for dogs when scared, jump like frogs.

E is for elephants and don't get it wrong, it's elephant not ephelant!

F is for flies, nuisances they can be, but it's sad when they die.

G is for giraffes, so tall you can't see their head,
  but can hear them laugh.

H is for hippos, they love the water and love going for dippoes!

I is for iguanas, well what can I say, they act like they're in a sauna.

J is for jaguars, fierce cats of the jungle,
  their eyes the colour of aqua!

K is for kangaroos and when they jump
  they'll say good day or toodle-loo.

L is for lions, and let me tell you their roar can shatter iron!

M is for monkeys, so cheeky and funny, but can be quite funky!

N is for newts, slimy and horrid, hmmm,
  a pet newt could be quite cute.

O is for ostrich, they're just so fast,
  30 secs and they're across the pitch!

P is for parrots, they can see so well, yet they don't eat carrots.

Q is for quails and watch out when they wail!

R is for rhinos I think they're descendants of dinos!

S is for snakes and for goodness sake,
  don't stroke them with a rake!

T is for tigers and when he's in love with a she
  he goes and sits beside her.

U is for urchins, small and deadly, in the deep they go lurching!

V is for vultures and raw meat is their culture.

W is for whale, blue or killer or one with a long tail!

X couldn't find an animal beginning with X. Do you know any?

Y is for yak, another wild beast, don't try and shave it, or it will attack.

Z is for zebras, full of fun and I know one whose name is Debra!

Yasmin Omar (10)
Holy Cross Preparatory School

Animals

Animals, weird things aren't they?
Some go baa, others go moo,
Some just go chew, chew, chew
Either way the same rule applies
What comes out of their behinds
1. It's got to be smelly
2. It's just like their belly!

Which rumbles, ev'ry stinkin' hour!
And ev'ry hour makes me cower,
At the sound it makes that very hour
So come on, let's read it again
Just before we reach
The end.

Maria Ojeda (11)
Holy Cross Preparatory School

Love

When you have found love,
You can almost feel the sky above,
Family and friends, relatives too,
They will always help you,
Through and through.

Friends forever, keeping secrets,
Sleepovers, parties, you reveal the deepest,
Cringes, crushes,
Lovers too,
They will always help you,
Through and through.

Families are the ones who are there,
Throughout our lives just to care,
Brothers and sisters, cousins too,
They will always help you,
Through and through.

Catriona Cahill (10)
Holy Cross Preparatory School

Happiness

Happiness is yellow like the sunset going down slowly.
It looks like yellowy-orangey paint splashed onto paper.
It feels like the sun is coming down to grab you.
It sounds like the hotness from the sun is screaming for you.
It tastes like a red-hot chilli pepper put into your mouth.
It smells like melting chocolate in your mouth straight from the fridge.
It reminds me of playing in the sea on the hottest day of the year.

Megan Hoey (9)
Holy Family Catholic Primary School

Anger

Anger is red like a scarlet dragon, breathing its blistering flames.
Anger feels like I'm holding the sun in the palm of my hand.
Anger smells like the scent of blood in the red sea.
Anger sounds like the cruel laugh of the Devil.
Anger tastes like chillies grown at the Earth's core.
Anger looks like an exploding petrol station.
Anger reminds me of a raging bull from Hell.

Declan Gwynne (9)
Holy Family Catholic Primary School

Fun

Fun is orange like the nose of a happy clown,
running around making children laugh.
It sounds like children running around throwing water bombs,
all blown up ready to burst.
It feels like a ball of happiness bursting inside your body
and makes you feel like all your worst thoughts
have been blown away.
It tastes like the sweetest strawberry,
smothered in chocolate sauce and sweet sugar.
It reminds me of the orange sunset, as beautiful as can be.
It smells like warm, melting chocolate in a saucepan.
It looks like a funny clown, throwing custard pies at his friend,
making them laugh.

Yolanda Seymour (9)
Holy Family Catholic Primary School

Hunger

Hunger is grey like an empty
rationing bowl being held out for food.

Hunger tastes like a plain, dull gravel
grinding away at your teeth
and sifting in your mouth.

Hunger smells like a piece of
old, soggy material that has
been dragged through a puddle
and then wrapped around you.

Hunger reminds me of a white
hungry seagull beckoning for
food with its screech and its scratch.

Hunger looks like a chalkboard
that hasn't been dusted, old, chalky and grey.

Hunger feels like someone stabbing
you in the stomach again and again,
clutching your tummy you beg for mercy.

Hunger sounds like someone beating
a drum inside your head, drumming
and drumming it into your brain so that
you can't forget that you are hungry.

Tyler Smith (10)
Holy Family Catholic Primary School

Silence

The grey silence is like a cold, jagged stone
cutting deep wounds in your hands.

Silence sounds like an eerie, low, non-stop hum
that has no end.

The smell of silence is like a deep pit of nothingness
that overfills your nostrils.

Silence reminds me of a lonely, desolate child,
weeping all alone.

Tasting silence is like tasting a recent, fresh pile of ash,
collected from a terrible fire.

When you touch silence you feel empty,
except for the miserable memories playing inside your head.

If you ever get to see silence, you will know that it is
like a transparent curtain that surrounds you everywhere you go.

Rebeca Escorihuela (10)
Holy Family Catholic Primary School

Laughter

Laughter is the colour orange.
It is like the bright, burning sand on the sandy beach.

Laughter looks like the Sahara Desert,
In the burning, blistering, scorching sun.

Laughter smells like wind rushing through the air,
The salty water in the baby-blue sea calm, not rough.

Laughter tastes like sweet popcorn
Popping in the oven and crunching in your mouth.

Laughter sounds like palm trees swishing side to side
In the 100°C sun.

Laughter reminds me of when I went to Spain
And had a wonderful time.

Laughter feels like cold ice in a freezer,
Cracking the glass.

Alfie Deacon (9)
Holy Family Catholic Primary School

Happiness

Happiness shares the colour of *yellow*,
Like the sunbeams stretching to reach you.

Happiness *smells* like the gorgeous
Smell of an extra chocolate doughnut.

Happiness *tastes* like some juicy ribs
With the sauce melting in your mouth.

Happiness *feels* like your mother's open heart
As she grabs you and cuddles you tight.

Happiness *sounds* like children laughing
As they splash into a crystal clear blue pool.

Happiness *reminds* me of a child's first step
And a beam on their face appears.

Sofia Rodrigues (10)
Holy Family Catholic Primary School

Anger

Anger is crimson-red like a boiling spark
flowing through the midnight sky.
Anger tastes like deep blue ink,
rushing down your throat and deep into your heart.
Anger reminds me of burning flames
falling down a pit to nowhere.
Anger smells like cloudy smoke
struggling to get down your nostrils.
Anger feels like a sprig of holly being pushed
deep into your soul and leaving a permanent dent.
Anger sounds like the sizzle of a candle
as a drop of water is poured onto it.
Anger looks like a deep sly grin
as you make a masterplan to hurt someone.

Alex Trigg (10)
Holy Family Catholic Primary School

Silence

Silence is deep grey like a forever-lasting path
leading to nothing.

Silence smells like the fresh, salty sea swaying in the distance
as you walk along the golden, sandy beach shore.

Silence sounds like a peaceful grave on a winter's night
in a faraway island.

Silence makes me feel like floating away to Sleep City
and never coming back.

Silence reminds me of a house when all are away,
going on a long journey to Sleep City.

Daniella Federico (10)
Holy Family Catholic Primary School

Sadness

Sadness is blue,
blue like the swaying, salty sea.

Sadness looks like a red ribbon
on a branch, swaying in the breeze.

Sadness reminds me of blue raindrops
trickling on the flowers.

Sadness sounds like a newborn baby
crying for its mother who never comes near.

Sadness tastes like plain water,
still in a glass, not moving at all.

Sadness feels like gentle silk.

Sadness smells like a burning
BBQ on a summer's day.

Jodie O'Neill (10)
Holy Family Catholic Primary School

Sadness

Sadness is blue,
Blue as the ice-cold sea.

It reminds me of the salty sea,
when you are striding along the beach.

It feels like raindrops,
splashing on your hands.

It smells like salt
from the ocean itself.

It sounds like a baby
crying for its food.

It looks like a blue ribbon
swaying in the wind.

It tastes like salty water,
purified from the ocean.

Luke O'Brien (10)
Holy Family Catholic Primary School

Silence

Silence is cold, grey like a dead, crying graveyard.
Silence sounds like a baby being rocked to sleep
by his mother's tender arms.
Silence looks like a caterpillar wrapped in a silken cocoon,
ready to turn into a beautiful butterfly.
Silence feels like a newborn baby wrapped in silken covers,
freshly made by silkworms.
Silence smells like winter's here, the ice-cold
blistering coldness fighting with you.
Silence reminds me of my baby brothers asleep.

Sacha Clayton (10)
Holy Family Catholic Primary School

Happiness

Happiness is yellow like a gleaming golden bird.
Happiness tastes like gorgeous blackcurrant medicine
that Mum gives me when I'm ill.
Happiness sounds like a mermaid, beautifully singing
on a lonely rock in the middle of the sea.
Happiness reminds me of a gleaming angel up in Heaven.
Happiness smells like Grandma's home-baked cookies.
Happiness feels like a beautiful light bulb,
brighter than all the rest inside of me.
Happiness looks like the shiny sun with a smile on its face.

Jake Aldridge (10)
Holy Family Catholic Primary School

Sadness

Sadness is the colour of the soft cloudy skies,
it reminds me of a quiet ocean, rushing very gently and quietly.

Sadness feels soft like blue silk running through your fingers,
slowly and steadily.

The smell of something rich baking in the oven,
something like chocolate biscuits.
That's what I think smells of sadness, do you?

It tastes like a Galaxy, melting in your mouth
again and again!

And sadness sounds like church bells,
far, far in the distance.

Sadness looks like a ribbon blowing gently in the soft breeze,
that makes the sand on the beach blow around softly.

Clare Walmsley (9)
Holy Family Catholic Primary School

Hunger

Hunger is grey like a
Thundery cloud on a
Dull, bleak winter's day.

It feels as empty as
A crumpled old paper,
Sweet wrapper floating
Calmly in the air,
As quiet as a dragonfly.

It tastes like a bitter lime
In the bottom of a fruit bowl,
Hiding.

It sounds like a rumbling,
Golden tambourine
In someone's stomach.

It reminds me of stones,
Galloping along the
Gleaming, sandy beach.

It smells like a dragon's
Steaming, foul breath,
Trying to attack someone.

Hannah Russell (9)
Holy Family Catholic Primary School

Laughter

Laughter is yellow like the bright burning sand
on a sandy beach, that makes the beach joyful and happy.

The laughter feeling is like an Easter new chick,
smooth, silky yellow that slips from hand to hand.

Laughter sounds like a circus as a clown struts his marvellous jokes,
as he and the audience laugh and laugh all day.

A reminder of laughter to me is of the sun dancing in the air,
through massive, so soft, delicate and bouncy clouds.

The lovely smell of laughter is like a beautiful, most fragrant flower,
beaming and smiling in the sun.

I imagine laughter to taste like a boiled, juicy melon and
strawberry sweet, slowly melting in my mouth.

I think laughter would look like a bright, yellow-orange bouncy ball,
bouncing on a lovely beach on a summer's day.

Madeleine Harding (9)
Holy Family Catholic Primary School

Sadness

The colour of the sky,
blue on the windiest day of the year.

It reminds me of salty sea
while you are striding along the beach.

It feels like cotton wool
falling apart in your hands.

It smells like the salt
that has been tipped out.

It sounds like a baby crying out
for his favourite toy.

It looks like the beautiful sun
coming up over the sea.

It tastes like a freshly-opened chocolate bar
melting in your mouth.

Ryan East (9)
Holy Family Catholic Primary School

Anger

Anger is red like a hot sun about to burst.
Anger looks like a big rock that will never crack.
Anger feels like a big ball of fire in your head that just won't go away.
Anger sounds like an elephant going up and down the stairs.
Anger smells like smoke from a forbidden fire.
Anger tastes like a sour sweet in your mouth and the taste just
won't go away.

Sophie Burge (10)
Holy Family Catholic Primary School

Fun

Fun is the colour of orange.

Fun Is children waiting impatiently
for a go on the newest ride at the funfair.

Fun looks like a waxy peel of a ripe tangerine
sitting in a fruit bowl waiting to be eaten.

Fun smells like orange and chocolate swishing in a blistering
saucepan and the anticipation of waiting to eat it.

Fun tastes like a banana squelching in a mouth
liquidising into baby food.

Fun feels like a balloon floating up from your toes,
up to your brain, dodging this way and that.

Fun sounds like children laughing and chuckling,
after seeing a silly clown.

Fun reminds me of a spread of marmalade,
swiping the crusty, crumbly toast on a marble work surface.

Sophie Lightowlers (10)
Holy Family Catholic Primary School

The Day I Was Silly

When I was small,
Just eavesdropping on what my
Parents were saying,
I was
Very,
Very
Naughty!

I really didn't want to do it,
Really,
I hope you're not going to tell.

My mum
Wasn't letting my dad go to work,
So I hid his mobile and
Car keys!

I really didn't mean to do it,
Really,
Honest,
I'm innocent!

Daddy asked me
A few minutes later,
'Sadia, where are my car keys
And my mobile?'
I didn't answer him.
He said it again.
I still didn't answer.

Finally, after saying it yet again,
I answered, 'This time
I'm really innocent, I have no idea,
No idea, really.'
He really didn't believe me.

'Don't blame me!
I can't help it!'
I love being on Mum's side.
This time he has to believe me.
Well, he did,
After a few understandings.

We tried ringing with
Our home telephone.
We couldn't,
But as far as I am sure,
I know the car keys are
With the phone.
We tried the fourth time,
This time we could hear it.

It was under the table,
On top of the chair,
With the car keys
On a different chair.

They next thing they said was,
'Whatever you do,
Don't touch our stuff.'
I wanted to say something too,
'Whatever you do,
Do just listen to ladies!'

Sadia Ali (9)
Merland Rise Community Primary School

When I Broke A Window

Once,
When I was eight and a half,
I did something
That got me into
Lots
Of
Trouble
And gave me a *month* of misery.

I was up in my room,
Then I had an idea
Of how to get some fresh air.
I went in my mam
And dad's room and
Opened the window
And pushed
The back.
I then shut
The window
But I couldn't.
I forced
As hard
As I could
And I bent
The part
That opened the window
And stood as still as stone.
I ran downstairs
Told my mum and
My mum ran upstairs
And tried to fix it.

But couldn't.
I got my dad,
My dad said I was grounded -
For a month!
My dad fixed it
And I just cried!

Connor Harbour (8)
Merland Rise Community Primary School

My Naughty Poem

Once in my house,
When I was small,
Only one year old,
I did something
Very, very, very
Naughty.

Go on, I bet you've guessed.
OK, I'll tell you.
I wet myself
On the floor
Trying to get to the toilet in time.
This is how it all began.

I was dancing in the hall,
Then I decided I needed the toilet,
So I went to the stairs
And started to climb them.
Halfway, I had a little accident.
I stopped and looked,
I saw something wet.
I felt it was wee,
I had wet myself
On the new carpet.
I ran down the stairs,
I told my mum,
She went absolutely mad.
This is what she said,
'You bad girl,
Now in future
You tell me
When you need to go to the toilet.'
That is how it all happened.
I know what you're thinking,
What a naughty girl.
Maybe next time it
Won't be so bad,
But that's all for now,
Bye!

Jessica Monk (9)
Merland Rise Community Primary School

When I Was Naughty

Many years ago,
When I was just becoming four,
I did something,
Something
Very,
Very,
Naughty!

I didn't mean it,
I was just a curious girl.
My dad said, 'Don't run off.'
But I did, I ran off
In the car park.
I could hear Mum and Dad,
They were calling my name.
I thought that it would be fun
To go and see animals.
I could see my mum and dad,
They were coming closer.
'Shannon, are you here?'
I didn't reply,
I just carried on running!
But, I fell over
And my leg was bleeding!
Mum and Dad found me
And took me home.
Next time,
I won't run away!

Shannon Burnett (9)
Merland Rise Community Primary School

When I Was Naughty

Once, when I was six,
I did something
That was very naughty
(And I worried my parents!)

When I was in bed,
I thought about a plan
Going outside and camping.
Well, I was begging Mum and Dad
To go camping.

I got my dad to open my window
And I put my plan into action.
I got my duvet and pillow
Out of the window,
I put my slippers on
And went out of the window.

I held the part over the top
Of the window itself
And it crumbled away.
I jumped onto the grass
And set my duvet and pillow
Like a bed.

Minutes later, my mum
Turned on the light.
She went inside
And saw no Daniel.
She told Dad,
He shouted at me,
'Get inside!'
I went inside and
Knew I was in *deep*
Trouble!

I slept inside
And I never
Went camping again!

Daniel Linford (9)
Merland Rise Community Primary School

When I Was Naughty

When I was seven
I was
Very,
Very
Naughty!
I was
Playing catch
With my dad.
I threw
The ball
Too hard
And
Smash!
I'd broken
The shed
Window
Which
Made
My dad
Very,
Very
Cross!
Then he
Was chasing
Me around
The garden.
My dad said,
'Where is the tennis ball?'
'I don't know.'
I am going
To tell
My dad
Where
I put it.
Not!

Charlie Holt (9)
Merland Rise Community Primary School

When I Loved Ponies

Once, when I was only about six,
When I loved ponies,
I was
Very,
Very,
Bad!

When my mum said,
'Don't go on a pony yet!'
Mum was getting ice lollies.
I had money,
£2.50!
But then it was
My turn.
I bet you know,
I went on a
Big,
Tall,
Pony!

Thump.

I went on the stool,
There I was
On a black pony.
My mum looked
Very
Cross!

I got off
Looking sad.
'Where is my lolly?'
'You're in
Big,
Big
Trouble.'
'So.'
I think my mum has
Not
Forgotten that day!

Faith Ekpedekumo (9)
Merland Rise Community Primary School

When I Was Naughty

One day,
About four years ago,
I did something
Very,
Very
Naughty!
My mum got cross,
She hasn't recovered yet!

I wanted a hamster,
Really,
Really,
Badly!
My mum wouldn't get me one!
I threw a
Very,
Very
Big
Tantrum.
She still said no!

So, I waited until the builder came round,
Then I lured my mum, brother and
The builder into my room.
When they were talking,
I stepped out,
Locked the door
And smiled.

'Hey, let us out!'
'No.'
'I haven't done anything wrong.'
'It's your fault, you should have bought me a hamster!'
So I went into the front room,
Jumped onto the computer,
Couldn't care less.

Half an hour later:
'Hey, let us out now,
Your brother needs a drink and the toilet!'
'No. Well I might if you buy me a hamster!'

'Huh, OK.'
'Really?'
'Yes!'
So I let them out.
Guess how many hamsters I got?
Two!
I never locked anyone in a room,
Ever,
Ever,
Ever
Again!

Holly Royal (9)
Merland Rise Community Primary School

When I Was Naughty

When I was very small,
Quite young,
I was going out with my mum and dad
And I did something
Very,
Very,
Naughty!

I was going to have my
First ice cream!
When we were walking along
I stuffed the ice cream
In my face.
My mum told me off,
Then my dad said,
'Louise, we are not made of money
And we are not getting you
Another ice cream!'
And I am not going
To do that again.

Louise Corless (9)
Merland Rise Community Primary School

I Want My Lunch

When I was small,
(Only four),
I got grounded
For a month!
I was very,
Very naughty!
This is how
I got grounded.

On a Monday
I came downstairs
For lunch.
My dad wouldn't
Let me have lunch.

So I waited.
He went into
The kitchen,
So I ate
His sandwich.
'Why did you
Eat mine?'
'Because you
Won't let me
Have my
Lunch now!'

Ben Smith (9)
Merland Rise Community Primary School

The Day I Was Naughty

Once, when I just turned three,
I was really naughty.
I caused an accident,
Serious,
I was a very, very, very
Naughty boy!

I laid a rake
In the garden just before
My dad and brother
Started to do the gardening.

Argh!
Ouch!
It was my dad and my brother.
My dad stood on the rake and
Fell on my brother.
I started to laugh.
Ha, ha, ha, ha, ha, ha.
My dad and my mum came over to me.
'You naughty boy.'
'I didn't do anything.
It might not have been me,
It might have been Daniel.'
'No!
'Bradley,
It was you!
Otherwise, if it
Was Daniel,
He would tell me.'
'I'm sorry.'
'All right Bradley,
I understand.'

And anyway,
I can't do it again.
I live in a flat.
(I'm not really sorry for it,
I was joking.)

Bradley Beckett (8)
Merland Rise Community Primary School

Ever Since My Dad Moved Out!

Ever since Dad moved out
Mum hasn't been able to shout
Every single day they had a fight
All the way into the middle of the night.

When I used to go to bed
Dad always used to kiss me on the head
Dad bought me sweets every week
And we always used to play hide-and-seek.

When I get home from school
Dad isn't there at all.
Dad never comes home
And never answers his phone.

I never see my dad
And I'm very, very sad.

Ellie Grindrod (10)
Ridgeway Primary School

Summer

S ummer is a time for fun
U nder the tree is a beautiful butterfly
M eadows filled with wild flowers
M eandering rivers flow through the valleys
E leven bees annoying people having a picnic
R abbits hopping about having fun.

Lorna Clarke (10)
Ridgeway Primary School

Food, Glorious Food

Custard and toast,
I hate it the most.
Chocolate and bacon,
Never gets taken.
Fish in a dish and orange juice too,
I'll give you a clue, *no thank you!*
I don't want this,
It's far from bliss.
I scream for ice cream,
All sorts of allsorts and liquorice to chew.
Scrummy fudge and sticky toffee,
Not the sludge that is meant to be lamb stew.
So the next time you pick up your knife and fork,
Don't forget the poem that you've been taught,
Don't eat food of a peculiar kind,
You may find yourself in a whole new state of mind!

Alice West & Nicole Reid (10)
Ridgeway Primary School

Life Just Hasn't Been The Same!

Ever since the baby came, life just hasn't been the same.
Of course at first she slept a lot,
Of course I wasn't allowed to make any noise in case she woke,
Playing quietly is no joke.
We soon found out about all the fuss,
The baby seemed to make more noise than us!

At tea time from her chair she threw her tea everywhere,
Peas and potatoes went whizzing, my head starting spinning.
My dad and I soon learnt how to duck.
My mum said with any luck, 'She'll soon be past this stage
And life will be the same.'

She's yapping now and drives me dotty,
Sitting down on her potty,
She wants me to come and play,
But I say, 'No, maybe another day.'
She's even repeating every word I say.
She's moving my stuff everywhere
And even says, 'I don't care!'
Will life ever be the same?

Sakilé Williams-Ofari-Atta (10)
Ridgeway Primary School

Global Warning

The Earth has put her suncream on
Her face is going pink,
But nobody will listen,
They won't just stop and think.
Her snowy hair is melting
It might not grow again,
It's killing all the animals
It will kill all the men.
Her skin is getting wrinkled,
The silkiness is going,
Her happiness is ending
Her sorrow is now growing.
She longs for times gone past,
When she was only young,
When birds sat high up in leafy trees,
And through the day they sung:
Tweet, tweet the world is sweet,
We love to sing all day,
Cheep, cheep the world is sweet,
And now we shout, 'Hooray!'
There's no need to worry,
No time to fret,
You can still help
It's not over yet.

Rachel Hammond & Katie Tomsett (10)
Ridgeway Primary School

A Fox

Inside the fox's eye, the scampering rat.
Inside the scampering rat, the fox's feet.
Inside the fox's feet, the damp worm.
Inside the damp worm, the soft mud.
Inside the soft mud, the drips of water.
Inside the drips of water, the fox's cubs.
Inside the fox's cubs, the fox's eye.

William Hyde-East (8)
St Catherine's Primary School, Bletchingley

Dog

Inside the dog's eyes, the shining moonlight.
Inside the shining moonlight, the dog's scruffy fur.
Inside the dog's scruffy fur, the bushy forests.
Inside the bushy forests, the dog's pointed ears.
Inside the dog's pointed ears, the dangerous mountain.
Inside the dangerous mountain, the dog's sharp fangs.
Inside the dog's sharp fangs, the cat's blood.
Inside the cat's blood, the dog's tears,
Inside the dog's tears, the hunter's gun,
Inside the hunter's gun, the dog's eyes.

Georgina Allen (9)
St Catherine's Primary School, Bletchingley

Cat

Inside the cat's eyes a fiery, bright moon shines,
Inside the fiery, bright moon, the cat's gigantic claws,
Inside the cat's gigantic claws, a lake of water,
Inside the lake of water, the cat's dim reflection,
Inside the cat's dim reflection, a mountain so high,
Inside the mountain so high, the cat's dry mouth,
Inside the cat's dry mouth, a squeak of panic,
Inside the squeak of panic, the cat's pink, wet nose,
Inside the cat's pink, wet nose, a glorious sunset,
Inside the glorious sunset, the cat's eyes.

Louise Hearn (9)
St Catherine's Primary School, Bletchingley

Monkey

I see a monkey swinging tree to tree
I see the monkey in a banana tree
Looking for a banana in the tree
Then the monkey eating his banana, slowly in the tree
I see the monkey looking down at me
Then he drops his banana and comes over to me
He puts his hands on the cage with a sad face
With a tear in his eye, I feel sorry for him
I let him free.

Rudi Skilton (9)
St Catherine's Primary School, Bletchingley

Gorilla

Gorilla, gorilla black as night
Gorilla, gorilla ready for the fight
Gorilla, gorilla full of might
Other gorillas full of fright
They can never overcome his might.

Benton White (9)
St Catherine's Primary School, Bletchingley

My Puppy

Inside me I feel a little tingle of a puppy
Bouncing for joy, I feel it coming out
How would I know (what is right or wrong)?
I know I can go, but what if I don't
What would happen if I go?
I don't want to go
What will I do?
To make myself not go
I wish I'm at home.

Katie Field (8)
St Catherine's Primary School, Bletchingley

Lion

Inside the lion's claw, the curved boomerang,
Inside the curved boomerang, the lion's tail,
Inside the lion's tail, the sharp jaw,
Inside the sharp jaw, the lion's shaggy mane,
Inside the lion's shaggy mane, the zebra's tear,
Inside the zebra's tear, the lion's paw,
Inside the lion's paw, the lion's whiskers,
Inside the lion's whiskers, the lion's claw.

Ryan Hutson (9)
St Catherine's Primary School, Bletchingley

Rhodesian Ridgeback

Inside the ridgeback's powerful jaw, the big powerful teeth.
Inside the powerful teeth, the lion's cry.
Inside the lion's cry, the tall grass.
Inside the tall grass, the ridgeback's golden fur.
Inside the ridgeback's golden fur, the ridgeback's blood.
Inside the ridgeback's blood, the strong bones.
Inside the strong bones, the powerful jaw.

Reece Allen (9)
St Catherine's Primary School, Bletchingley

Wolf

Wild winds roar as an owl swoops on the wolf
Lurking in the white snow
Frost is coming
Run wolf run
Inside me is the snow that the wolf is calling
Perma frostbite
Inside the powerful frostbite, the wolf getting attacked
Inside the wolf getting attacked
The wolf lying on the snow, dead.

Daniel Lobley (9)
St Catherine's Primary School, Bletchingley

I Have A Dream

I have a dream, that all people will be equal,
No need for fire arms to be carried,
Heaven.

I have a dream, that violence won't be tolerated,
No need for people to envy others,
Heaven.

I have a dream, that respect will conquer every mind,
No starving people in Africa,
That is Heaven.

David Crowe (11)
St Catherine's Primary School, Bletchingley

Imagine If . . .

Imagine if . . .
No one was hungry
Everyone had enough food.

Imagine if . . .
No one was homeless
Everyone had a home.

Imagine if . . .
No one was thirsty
Everyone had enough water.

Imagine if . . .
All children had toys and presents
And lived lives happily.

Imagine if . . .
No one was afraid
No violence and murders in the world.

Imagine if . . .
There were no racist attacks
Everyone living in peace.

Imagine if . . .
My dream came true.

Danny Love (10)
St Catherine's Primary School, Bletchingley

I Have A Dream

I have a dream . . .

That war is over,
Nothing will make it come back,
We can stick together,
The perfect world

I have a dream . . .

That there will be no hunger,
No more unhealthy water to drink,
We all must use our food wisely,
The perfect world.

I have a dream . . .

There's no more hatred,
Just love and caring,
We share the things we have equally,
The perfect world.

I have a dream . . .

There's no difference between black and white,
And no killing because of colour,
Black and white children play happily together,
The perfect world.

I have a dream . . .

Lauren Ball (10)
St Catherine's Primary School, Bletchingley

The Wind

I can blow things over
I can be really nasty
I am the worst destroyer
I can be gentle and calm
I can be a sweet little breeze
I start tornadoes and hurricanes
And I like to destroy your sunny days
What am I?

Charlotte Fisher (11)
St Catherine's Primary School, Bletchingley

Nature Is . . .

Nature is a flower shedding its petals of beauty,
Nature is the sun blasting life on Earth,
Nature is Man peacefully living side by side with animals in harmony,
Nature is a work of art, perfected over millions of years.
Nature is animals embedding themselves in the earth.
Nature is Man living and breathing on Earth.

Brett Fuller (11)
St Catherine's Primary School, Bletchingley

Who Am I?

Who am I?

I live in the soil
And I cry, cry and cry,
No memory, no legs, no friends,
My mum doesn't love me,
The message she sends.

Who am I?

I have no food
But I try, try, try,
My enemy is birds,
I slither away when they emerge.

Who am I?

I wish I could tell you,
I can't give a clue,
I don't say anything,
But I wish I could sing.

Rebecca Ward-Morris (11)
St Catherine's Primary School, Bletchingley

Imagine

Imagine a world with no greed, no selfishness, no hate.
Imagine a world with enough food for everyone to survive.
Imagine a world with no murders, no racism, no envy.
Imagine a world with no people who want more.
Imagine a world without Pandora's Box.

James Hearn (11)
St Catherine's Primary School, Bletchingley

If . . .

If there were no poverty,
The world would be halfway there.
If we shared our food - money,
Africans would not starve.

If there were no war,
Population would be an 1/8th up.
If we persuade, talk and think,
Billions more would live.

If there were no prejudice,
We would all get along.
Everyone would live in peace,
And most wars would cease to exist.

If there were no disasters,
Another 1/8th would be saved.
Although it is not our doing,
It still wrecks the world.

If we all had respect,
The world would be perfect.
Like a dream coming true,
But it is still far away.

Ben Malaihollo-Sheppard (10)
St Catherine's Primary School, Bletchingley

I Have A Dream

I have a dream,
Will it come true?
No war, no violence,
People living in peace,
I have a dream,
Wouldn't it be great?

I have a dream,
That everyone will have homes to go to,
No one crying because they're cold,
I have a dream,
Wouldn't it be great?

I have a dream,
Will it come true?
No water shortages,
No people dying or begging for water,
I have a dream,
Wouldn't it be great?

I have a dream,
That there are no terrorists,
No murderers, no rapists,
I have a dream,
Wonderful wouldn't it be?

Aimee Hill (11)
St Catherine's Primary School, Bletchingley

I Have A Dream

I have a dream . . .

I have a dream to live in peace,
No fighting, no killing.

I have a dream for everyone to have the same rights,
No name calling, no prejudice,
No fights because of the colour of our skin.

I have a dream for everybody to share,
So people in Africa don't die of starvation,
So people don't cry themselves to sleep.

I have a dream for people to love,
Love not hate,
People love but they hate.

I have a dream or I did.

Ashley Walker (11)
St Catherine's Primary School, Bletchingley

My Dream

Imagine there's no war,
People dying for our own greed.
Why not just get on, make the world a better place
I have a dream!
I hope it comes true!

Imagine there's no bullying,
Children's lives get ruined by children not caring about others.
This is my dream!

Imagine there's no weapon,
No one would need one for the war has ended,
So my dream is coming true,
So keep dreaming with me!

Abigail Church (11)
St Catherine's Primary School, Bletchingley

Cat

Inside the cat's teeth, the blood of a mouse.
Inside the blood of a mouse, the sharp whiskers.
Inside the sharp whiskers, a bird's cry.
Inside a bird's cry, the cat's powerful feet.
Inside the cat's powerful feet, the razor-sharp claws.
Inside the razor-sharp claws, the fly's wings.
Inside the fly's wings, the bony leg.
Inside the bony leg, the cat's heart.
Inside the cat's heart, the cat's life.
Inside the cat's life, the cat's energy.
Inside the cat's energy, the skin of a mouse.
Inside the skin of a mouse, the cat's teeth.

Connie Howard (9)
St Catherine's Primary School, Bletchingley

I Have A Dream

I have a dream,
That one day,
We will live
In peace and harmony.

I have a dream,
That doesn't exist,
Work together
And change this life.

I have a dream,
That there will be
No war, no greed and no anger.

I have a dream,
That there's no terrorists
And no July the 7th bombing
And no more killing one another.

I have a dream,
Everyone sharing food,
Water and clothing.

I might not know everything,
But I do know one thing,
That all should be treated with respect
And all are equal.

Charlotte Worcester (11)
St Catherine's Primary School, Bletchingley

Elephant

Inside the elephant's tusks, the tree,
Inside the tree, the tree's twigs,
Inside the tree's twigs, the tree's leaves,
Inside the tree's leaves, the elephant's teeth,
Inside the elephant's teeth, the bark of a tree,
Inside the bark of a tree, the dust storm,
Inside the dust storm, the elephants,
Inside the elephants, the grass,
Inside the grass, the marsh,
Inside the marsh, the rocks,
Inside the rocks, the elephant's trunk,
Inside the elephant's trunk, water,
Inside the water, the elephant's tusks.

Tom Critchley (9)
St Catherine's Primary School, Bletchingley

Better World

I have a dream; there are no wars
No fighting nor hatred,
Stop the hatred and war.

I have a dream; there's no racism,
Black and white shall unite,
Live together in peace.

I have a dream; there's no greed,
Everyone has equal food and water,
There is plenty for mankind.

I have a dream; there's no murder,
No stabbing, no shooting,
The world is horrid.

Danny Booth (11)
St Catherine's Primary School, Bletchingley

The Sky

The sky is a perfect blue,
The weather begins to dramatically change,
The horizon turns crimson red,
The clouds start to gather,
Drowning the blood-ridden sky,
Replacing loss with anger.

Liam Field
St Catherine's Primary School, Bletchingley

Hurricanes And Breezes

I can be a howling, prowling monster,
Or nothing more than a soft breeze.

Tearing turf from their roots, houses lie in debris,
Anything in my path will be devastated in a cataclysmic way
Prowling and searching for houses to devastate.

We come in huge storms or in soft summer breezes.

I can be as soft and delicate to only ripple through the flowers
And carry off any dead petals using a single breath.

I can be a howling, prowling monster,
Or nothing more than a soft breeze.

Joshua Bell (11)
St Catherine's Primary School, Bletchingley

Leopard

Leopard,
Royal king of the wild.
Two-metre long compact body.
Leopard's majestic body,
Creeping through the dark of the night.
Silky, soft fur coat,
Spotted with every spot that the world can provide.
Muscular legs pulling its prey up the tree.
Small, sharp stones flying through the air,
Driving the leopard down.
Leopard striped of his self respect.
How long is it until the whole species is wiped out?

Oliver Newport (11)
St Catherine's Primary School, Bletchingley

Many Faces Of Wind

The wind is a clutching hand,
Tearing the sleeping, fallen leaves from their peaceful rest,
Mocking young and defenceless plants into gloomy, bitter corners.

The wind is a thief,
Slipping through every space he can possibly find,
Stealing umbrellas, hats and scarves from unwatching eyes,
Fishing bulbs out of the warm, soft earth,
'You are useless,' he sniggers.

The wind is a balloon,
Uncontrollably fast as he thunders along,
Aggressively controlling the string as the wind controls the leaves,
Through cloud and sky he dashes.

The wind is a humble mother,
Gently polishing petals of delicate grace,
Weaving in and out of them
So as not to wake them from their dreamy sleep,
A smooth summer breeze tugs at your hair,
A cool scentless breath of wind that floods your face,

This is the wind with its many faces!

Seanne Kohler (11)
St Catherine's Primary School, Bletchingley

Imagine

Imagine there's no greed,
No more hunger in Africa.

I wonder if it will come true,
Do you too?
I wonder if the world will change in one day.

Imagine there's no envy,
No stealing other people's possessions.

I wonder if it will come true,
Do you too?
I wonder if the world will change in one day.

Imagine there's no war,
No families being killed.

I wonder if it will come true,
Do you too?
I wonder if the world will change in one day.

Imagine there's no prejudice,
No racist attacks and suicide.

Harry O'Leary (11)
St Catherine's Primary School, Bletchingley

Forget-Me-Not

Forget-me-not, forget-me-not
Please forget-me-not
You're better than
The foxglove or freesia

Forget-me-not, forget-me-not
Please forget-me-not
Bring back my most
Picturesque dream

Forget-me-not, forget-me-not
Please forget-me-not
Help me remember
My family when they die

And please, oh please, forget-me-not
Make sure you forget-me-not.

Elizabeth Williams (11)
St Catherine's Primary School, Bletchingley

The Wind

I can be a calm breeze when I want to be,
But do not offend me,
Most of my victims come off second best,
Sometimes I can be as cold and prickly as a cactus,
Or as calm as a mid summer's day,
But whenever police are looking for suspects,
I just vanish . . .
Like the wind.

Isobel Ruffle (10)
St Catherine's Primary School, Bletchingley

The Invisible Riddle

I am a thief, stealing things I do not need,
I sweep and swipe the roads, clean to suit your satisfaction,
I do not get paid, yet I still work all hours, unable to stop,
I work in silence and secretly ignored by passing pedestrians,
I am the unknown stranger but yet so common,
I can also cause destruction and devastation,
I can create cataclysmic changes in all elements,
I howl for my cousins, brothers and sisters to gather in my storm,
I bellow a hollow cry announcing my unleashed anger,
Yet I can be gentle and calming and soothe your skin,
I can breathe rhythmic bursts of warm air to comfort,
When will I be noticed . . .
. . . Never
I am the invisible riddle.

Thomas Mulligan (11)
St Catherine's Primary School, Bletchingley

My World Of Fantasy

I was sucked into a world,
Of total make-believe,
Everything was so cold,
I was hungry for my tea,
It's simply impossible,
To know that it wasn't actually me,
I know it isn't real,
But I truly wish it was,
I can sometimes feel,
The mystery and guess,
Believing in total fantasy,
Making me believe in magic,
And some things extraordinary,
Maybe something tragic,
Could make someone happy,
Or maybe even sad,
It's a shame, I could be a happy chappy,
Or a sad loser,
But that's me I suppose,
Just plain, old, boring me.

Katherine Gilbert (11)
St Thomas of Canterbury School, Guildford

Cars

So fast, so quick.
If you need, take your pick.

Exceptionally nice, ever so sleek,
You might just want to take a peek.

On the track like going into space,
You might just find yourself in 1st place!

When you're in the driver's seat, looking through the smoke,
If you make it to the last lap; don't choke.

Toby Eden (10)
St Thomas of Canterbury School, Guildford

The Room

I step into the room,
I hear a *boom!*
I turn to the left,
A TV screen,
Is what I have seen.

I look right,
A desk and a chair,
I look in front and get a scare,
A monster, dripping in goo,
I stand there dumbstruck, don't know what to do.

I start to move back,
The door has changed,
I really think this is quite deranged,
I try the lock
And run for my life,
If I tell anyone, they'll just mock.

Dominic Male (11)
St Thomas of Canterbury School, Guildford

Zoo

Went to a zoo,
parked the car,
walked to the entrance,
which was very far!

Monkeys first,
who are very funny,
out in the enclosure,
which is very sunny!

Next the birds,
flying all around,
as if never wanting
to touch the ground!

Finally the big cats,
tigers and lions too,
roaring everywhere,
around the zoo!

In the end,
we went home,
not forgetting,
our ice cream cone!

Lawrence Bird (11)
St Thomas of Canterbury School, Guildford

My Old World War II

Run, run, run away,
daylight by moonlight,
day by day.
Past the old farmhouse,
where there used to be guns,
at that point armies did not have much fun.
Down by the lake,
big holes lay in the ground,
where the bombs had fallen down.
Past that, an Anderson shelter does lie,
that saved some people,
they did not die.
That's the end of my World War II,
but there are many more things,
and much more to do.

Emma Sewell (11)
St Thomas of Canterbury School, Guildford

Awesome Athletics

Athletics is a very superb sport
I'm always on the run
And always having fun, fun, fun
Whenever I do high jump
I seem to end up with a bump
When I do the shot-put
I always move my foot
And I get a foul throw
Then I come last in the show
But I don't really care
As I have played fair
And when you compete
Don't ever cheat!

Vicky Maguire (11)
St Thomas of Canterbury School, Guildford

People

Some people are little, some people are large,
Some people even live on a barge.

Some live in deserts, some live in snow,
Some people live nowhere and have nowhere to go.

Some people are famous, some people are rich,
A few of them play on a football pitch.

Some people have wars, some people have fights,
Sometimes they can go on for endless nights.

Some people are bad, some people are mean,
But some nice people might buy you an ice cream!

Dylan Bonds (11)
St Thomas of Canterbury School, Guildford

A Superhero

When pigs can fly,
I'll cry,
For I'm Super Circle!
Let villains fear
When I'm here!
Member of the Thick Three
Hmm hmm . . . don't you mean leader
Of the Thick Trio!
My name . . .
I cannot say!
X-ray showed
Brain the size of a:
A) Elephant
B) Monkey
C) Pea.
Correct answer is:
C) A pea.
Accomplices:
Fudge Square,
Onreco Elocos Romeo Ramhos Halocos,
Aka Chuck
Join Now.

William Gifford McGuiness (11)
St Thomas of Canterbury School, Guildford

Friendships

F riends are super-dooper
R ather cool
I n my new class pool
E nding the day with loads of giggles
N othing to do but chat, chat, chatter
D om came in and ruined our game
S illy boy, who likes him? (He's my brother, so I love him really!)
H ip, hop we're bobbing to the music
I n the lounge watching TV
P eople come in, we smile sweetly
S oon as they've gone we're up to no good.
  What would I do without my friends?

Bethany Newman (11)
St Thomas of Canterbury School, Guildford

Running

The nerves are building
For the big race,
Lining up at the start
Everyone telling you to run at your own pace.

Ready at the start
Can't wait to get going,
Last run of the season
Oh no! not that annoying thing.

The gun goes up
I hate the loud bang,
Nearly four laps round the track
Before you know it, the bell starts to clang.

The final lap comes around
Your legs start to ache,
The finish is in sight
But it's first place I take.

Daniel Price (11)
St Thomas of Canterbury School, Guildford

Magical World Of Books

Books take me into different worlds.
They take me into boarding schools with lots of girls.
They make me believe in wizardry and magic.
Some stories can be scary, maybe even tragic.
I get sucked into a different adventure every time.
Some books have poems and I like poems with rhyme.
Some people think reading is boring and is a waste of time,
But reading is a favourite hobby of mine!

Jade Coombes (10)
St Thomas of Canterbury School, Guildford

The Beach - Haikus

Footsteps in the sand
As I walk along the beach
Footsteps in the sand

Kids come out to play
The day starts over again
Kids come out to play

Collecting all shells
Varied shape, colours, sizes
Collecting all shells

We're digging away
With many buckets and spades
We're digging away

The sun's going down
Whilst the waves wash up pebbles
The sun's going down

The fun has been had
We are now on our way home
The fun has been had.

Hannah Gibbs (11)
St Thomas of Canterbury School, Guildford

Hobbies

My favourite hobby is football
And yes, it is so cool.

My main position is in goal
I have most of the control.

Sometimes I play in defence
But it can get terribly tense.

Football can be very fun
Unless you're losing twenty to one.

Next on the list comes netball
It can be fun for all.

My main position varies a lot
So sometimes I can have a shot.

My worst position is goalkeeper
I'd rather be a carpet sweeper.

Sport is the best thing
The world could ever bring.

Grace Phelan (11)
St Thomas of Canterbury School, Guildford

Last Man Standing

Many aeons ago, a battle raged
Between those who were mortal and those who never aged.
Swords clashed and arrows flew
And even the strongest warriors were slew.
On the battlefield many fell,
Being there was like being in Hell.
On the enemy's side were shades of lore
But on the humans' side were dragons of four.
At the end of the battle, one man stood
The features on his face obscured by a hood.
And that man shall never sleep
And return to the battlefield only to weep.

Christopher Boyle (11)
St Thomas of Canterbury School, Guildford

Where Am I?

Where am I?
Am I here
Or am I there?
No one knows where.

Am I in a nose's nostrils
Or am I in space?
I smell something good,
Something on my face.

It must be jam,
Maybe I'm in the kitchen.
But it's not slimy,
It's something rhymy.

Am I in a supermarket
Or am I nowhere?
It's something rhymy not slimy,
Have a good guess.

Alex Lillistone (10)
St Thomas of Canterbury School, Guildford

Ice Hockey

Hard hitting
Fast shooting
Breathtaking
Puck shooting
Goal stealing
Fun playing
Fast skating
Fast puck hitting
Hardcore fighting.

Harri Jones (11)
St Thomas of Canterbury School, Guildford

Relatives

First there's the crying baby,
Then there's sissy sister,
And don't forget Larry, brother,
Then there's Mary, my mummy,
Daddy gets stressy,
Uncle's getting a lot of money,
Aunty's walking in the passageway
Shouting, 'Get out of the way.'
Granny's grumpy, watching 'O'Grady'
Grandpa saying, 'See you later.'

Julien Amoruso (10)
St Thomas of Canterbury School, Guildford

The Girls' Guide To Boys

What is a boy?
Some girls say they're cute.
I totally disagree.
No fashion sense - it's all football.
They run around shouting and scoring.
Then come back bringing in a smell.
No wonder we all cringe,
At least they change their shoes at break.
Shirts untucked and ultra-short ties,
Real short hair and scrubby knees.
Lots of scabs and cuts and bruises,
Always fighting, always biting.
Twelfths on all their meals.
I'd love to moan a little more,
Tell people what they're really like,
But got to go, I'm in a rush,
To meet a certain boy. *Ha! Ha!*

Philippa Juliff (11)
St Thomas of Canterbury School, Guildford

Football

My favourite sport is footie
My favourite team is Arsenal
When I score a goal
I go running down the pitch.

I drink a lot of water
Have a great time getting fit
The other team score
It's 1-1, *oh no!*

I score the winning goal
Everyone breaks into tears
We did it! We won!
We won the Champions Cup.

We laugh and cheer
And drink champagne
While the other team
Cry in pure pain.

We won!

Lily Burtness (10)
St Thomas of Canterbury School, Guildford

A Tornado

Water and wind mixed together,
Gives us a rather bad piece of weather.

It's like a gigantic, twisting funnel about to go . . .
It's like a vicious ocean in which you must row.

Round and round the tornado goes . . .
There goes the washing line and the clothes!

The devastation it can cause,
It's not a show so there's no applause.

It's currently in New Zealand,
Round half the world and it'll be in England.

The people in New Zealand scatter,
The sound of feet go pitter-patter.

The animals suddenly start to panic,
They start to flee (they're getting frantic).

The World Cup is soon on display,
Please be careful, the tornado's on its way.

Stuart Gray (11)
St Thomas of Canterbury School, Guildford

A Kenning

Rule breaker
Magic maker
Friend keeper
Cat owner
Broom flyer
Spell caster
School saver
Bad Luke Haver
Animal lover
Sport hater
Fun haver.

A: Mildred Hubble from 'The Worst Witch'
by Jill Murphy.

Michael Thornton (11)
St Thomas of Canterbury School, Guildford

The Fiery Dragon

I fly through the sky on outstretched wings,
From where I am, I can see everything.

When I'm on ground I stomp about,
'Help a dragon,' the people all shout.

My teeth are sharp as sabres,
My claws grip like a vice,
My whip-like tail is ready,
Don't dare attack me or be prepared to pay the price!

My fiery breath is scorching,
At a hundred thousand degrees,
It'll burn you to a cinder,
Then you'll float away in the breeze!

Where I live is simply best,
The deepest, darkest cave,
And if you come to visit,
You are truly, truly brave.

Don't ask me of my age,
I was hatched so long ago,
So don't be surprised,
To be honest, I don't know!

So now you know about me,
And how scary I can be,
It's time for me to go back home,
And enjoy my own company.

Tristan Pegg (11)
The Russell School

The Pig Chorus

Duke and Duchess of Pork are we,
No other mammals so pleasant to see.
None but we have noses like plugs,
We're stronger than a billion bugs.

Oinky, oinkedy, piggly sound,
We think no mammals but us are so round.
Oinky, oinkedy, piggly will,
We think so then and we thought so still!

Luise Johannis (10)
The Russell School

The Fox Chorus

Prince and Princess of the foxes are we
No other creatures so grand we see
None but we have a tail so red
With fluffy fur for a cosy bed.

Foxy Loxy so cunning and sly
Stalking animals creeping by
Foxy Loxy so cunning and sly
Leaping and sleeping all the way until nigh.

Laura Auton (10)
The Russell School

My Trip To School

This morning, as I was on my way to school
the world outside started behaving badly.
The birds spoke to the hedgehog
whilst the creatures danced for their king.
Trees were howling and shouting
while the sun beamed down.
Leaves raced to the bin,
saying, 'Don't put me in!'
The grass waved to the trees excitedly.
The angry wind shook the tall buildings.
As I reached school it all stopped.

Tia Donovan (11)
The Russell School

The Wild Side

This morning, as I was on my way to school
the weather started behaving badly.

The leaves waved to the wind racing through the trees.
The cars, coughing and spluttering, tried to push in the traffic.
The traffic lights changed their mind from red to green.
The squirrels danced and pranced around the trees.
The birds chattered and chattered.

As I jumped off the school bus the rain thumped
and threw itself to my feet.

Thyra Gibbs (11)
The Russell School

On My Way To School

This morning as I was on my way to school
the world outside started behaving badly.

The houses opened their big eyes with a stretch and a yawn.
In the breeze the trees shook in the morning wind.
The grass waved to the flowers and the bushes.
By the road the traffic lights ordered the cars around like policemen.
As the buses crawled amongst the busy traffic,
they sunk their heads and muttered,
'It's too early in the morning for this!'
But I carried on plodding all the way to school.
When I thought we were almost there I looked at the time.
10.30am - *late!*

Ciara Egan (10)
The Russell School

The Mad Morning

This morning as I was on my way to school,
The world outside was behaving badly.
The wind started to howl and whisper with the trees.
Flowers danced gracefully in the morning sun,
But outside the garden wall . . .
Cars and motorbikes, roaring with rage, pushed through the traffic.
Buggies strolled cheerlessly.
Chimneys smoked with anger burning up inside.
Yawning windows opened as the morning just began.
When I reached school and I was sitting in my seat;
The sun gave me a smile.

Sahra Nasr (10)
The Russell School

On My Way To School

This morning as I was on my way to school,
The world outside started behaving badly.
The cars began to scream and sneeze.
As the bus went past it grumbled and squealed
And the lorry beeped like one hundred trumpets.
The clouds jumped like sheep
While the crackling motorbike went past.
Later things calmed down
But just as I got to the playground
The bell called me into the classroom.

Ellie Morrissey (11)
The Russell School

The Words Of The One She Loved

These cold words draw in thee,
To a treacherous tale of mystery.

'Twas a foggy day,
In the cold, sinister May.

For all around her footsteps echoed,
Throughout the still wood a riddle emerged.

She fell silent and still,
Wondering about the cause of the kill.

The reason for this journey, the reason for this pain,
The reason for this heartbreak that she had just obtained.

The shrill noise wormed its way,
In and out through her brain.

It spoke aloud a terrible tale,
Of selfishness, greed and betrayal.

A man who was lost, to be no more,
A man who wanted everything and laid it past the law.

He got what he wanted and what he deserved,
He didn't say what was out there, he didn't give the word.

And now he tosses in eternal sleep,
In his memory trying to keep,

The mystery hidden down with him,
And no one to learn of his life of sin.

And now she knows this mystery,
She must be silenced for eternity.

But in her heart she will always see,
The one who she loved, forever to be.

Natalie Camara (11)
The Russell School

A Rainy Trip To School

Giggling mischievously, the wind and rain
dashed around the streets,
squashing the flowers as they chatted and gossiped.
The cars beat them off with a flick of their eyelids
and the traffic lights winked at them, sharing a secret.
The grass was flattened under the weight of the angry hailstones.
When I entered school the trees called 'goodbye' to me.

Charlotte Ashe (11)
The Russell School

The Outside World

This morning as I was on my way to school,
The outside world started behaving badly.
The sun laughed and smirked at his brothers and sisters, the clouds.
The trees stretched, having been awoken by the wind.
Motorbikes roared and screeched as they raced through the town.
Cars coughed and buses sneezed as they squeezed
                                                              through the angry traffic.
Then just as I reached the school gate,
Everything calmed down.
The outside world lay quiet as quiet.

Makeda Vidal (10)
The Russell School

The World Outside Started Behaving Badly

This morning as I was on my way to school,
The world outside started behaving badly.
The bushes danced to the wailing wind.
A squeaky bike passed by, moaning and groaning.
Buildings blinked and smiled as the sun showed her dress of fire.
Cars in traffic saying, 'Come on! Hurry along!'
A cut-down tree let out a loud yawn.
Motorbikes emitted an ear-splitting roar of triumph.
As I reached school, the rain started to cry,
As the leaves whispered, 'Good morning!'

Meriel Woolf (11)
The Russell School

My Journey To School

This morning on my way to school
The outside world sprang to life.
The trees danced as the wind flew by,
The bridge yawned tiredly whilst I walked under it.
Pushing past me, the wind tried to get to work,
The drips of the puddles clung to my shoes.
The clouds played footie, racing towards the sun, their goal.
The leaves were sky-diving from the great oak.
By the time I went into the classroom everything had died down,
But the day had just started living.

Freya Strutt (11)
The Russell School

Yellow

Yellow like mouldy cheese, that smells as bad as a dustbin,
Or a baby chick with very soft feathers.

Yellow like a crackling fire that burnt down my neighbour's fireplace,
Or a blazing sun.

Yellow like dirty popcorn that's on the floor of the cinema,
Or one of Van Gogh's beautiful sunflowers.

Yellow like mouldy keys, you don't want to touch,
Or a tawny owl that hoots.

Yellow like dirty chips being eaten by a three-year-old,
Or a golden rooster, showing off its feathers.

Emilie Cunning (9)
The Russell School

Red Like . . .

Red like the . . .
Oozing flesh that
Quivers through your body.

Red like a . . .
Rose standing tall
In the sun.

Red like a . . .
Drop of blood
That slithers down your skin.

Red like a . . .
Tarantula
That makes you jump and scream.

Red like a . . .
Lava lamp
That shines all night long.

Red like a . . .
Danger sign
That stayed there overnight.

Matthew Bartholomew (9)
The Russell School

Yellow Like . . .

Yellow as the bright sun
popping out from the mountain.

Yellow as dirty teeth
dropping out of someone's mouth.

Yellow like a lovely sunflower
coming out to play with the other sunflowers.

Yellow like lemons in a basket
ripening in the sun.

Hayleigh Gallimore (8)
The Russell School

Red

Red . . .

Like a shining ruby
or crawling ants.

Like a juicy apple
or a thorny rose.

As hot as fire
or fresh blood.

As tasty as salmon
or weird lips.

Like a beautiful sunset
or a squishy tomato.

As a stop sign
or a spicy pepper.

Samuel Turner (9)
The Russell School

Red

As maroon as oozing flesh
that quivers down your body,
or as brick-red as a rose
standing tall in the sun.

As cherry as a drop of blood
that slithers down your skin,
or as vermilion as a poppy,
opening to the sun.

As crimson as a tarantula
that makes you jump and scream
or as scarlet as a firework
that makes a wonderful gleam.

As ruby as a lava lamp
that shimmers through the night,
or a danger sign
that gives you a terrible fright.

Danny Knight (9)
The Russell School

Orange, Orange

Orange like . . .

A peeled juicy orange
Or rotten cheese.

Like lava
Or a mildewed carrot.

Like a fire
Or rotting fungi.

Like a sparkling firework
Or orange slime.

Like orange juice
Or an empty carton.

Like a dead leaf
Or a tin of mouldy beans.

Like an orange snake
Or orange mould.

Like an orange pencil
Or orange poison.

Soloman Rees-Jones (9)
The Russell School

White

White like the clouds in the fresh sky
The beautiful flower that's opening its petals
A candle on the table or a romance
The snow on Christmas Day
The special paper we have at school
The spooky ghosts at night
The white hailstones that fall from the sky
A scary avalanche falling on me.

Catherine Byrne-Clark (9)
The Russell School

Amber

Amber like . . .

the roaring fire
gleaming upon the night,

a tawny owl
that hoots inside the tree,

the blazing sun
that shines above the ground,

a newborn chick
that squeaks inside its egg,

a shiny sunset
shimmering in the sky,

sparkling Catherine wheels
spinning in the tree,

a long carrot
sitting in the ground,

a growing sunflower
beaming up above.

Sophie Smith (9)
The Russell School

Red Like . . .

Red like . . .
A drop of blood.

Red like . . .
A beautiful rose hanging off a plant.

Red like . . .
A shiny ruby in a shop.

Red like . . .
Fire from a volcano.

Red like . . .
A danger sign.

Harrison Reader (8)
The Russell School

Orange

Orange like . . .

A juicy orange
Sitting in a fruit bowl,

The orange shooting star
Going round the world,

The shining planet Pluto in space
That no one can see,

A flaming tiger that spins
As it pounces on an owl,

The boiling hot sun
Sitting in space really still,

A sunset
Sitting in the sky.

Ayman Nasr (8)
The Russell School

Red

Red is a huge pot of blood,
Or like a shimmering ruby.

Red like a flaming house,
Or a beautiful rose.

Red like a roaring fire engine,
Or a lovely toy.

Red like a red lorry that has crashed into a stop sign,
Or a gleaming Ferrari.

Red like a squashed tomato,
Or a shining strawberry.

Johannes Foot (9)
The Russell School

Yellow

Yellow like a beautiful banana that is being scoffed.
As yellow as a scary fire's flame.
Yellow like a growing sunflower that rises out of the sun.
As yellow as the glowing sun that glows in the sky.
Yellow like hair that is nice and yellow.
As yellow as horrible dirty teeth that are yucky.
Yellow like a tiger that goes roar.

Kate Quest (9)
The Russell School

Red

Red like the blood from someone who has been badly injured
Or a field of lovely roses in a row.

Red like the blazing fire that burnt a very posh house
Or a very nice sunset.

Red like the dangerous lava coming out of the volcanoes
Or someone putting on red lipstick.

Red like squashed and mouldy tomatoes
Or a bright red coloured pencil being used by a girl.

Red like a blood python
Or a happy and blushing child.

Rana El-Hoshi (9)
The Russell School

Pink

Pink like a beautiful rose
Smelling sweetly

Pink like a tasty raspberry
Tasting really good

Pink like a beautiful butterfly
Flying in the air

Pink like sweet Piglet
Seeing Pooh Bear

Pink like a new baby
About to arrive

Pink like loving Valentine's Day
Hugs and kisses to everyone

Pink like some pretty cheeks
Sparkle all day

Pink like lips
Talking all day

Pink like a hand
Of a new baby

Pink like a guitar
Playing in the sun.

Molly Vine (8)
The Russell School

Dolphin, Dolphin

Dolphin, dolphin, as you see,
dolphin, dolphin in captivity.

Dolphin, dolphin, past his prime,
soon it'll be the end of time.

Dolphin, dolphin weeping at night,
his shiny silhouette bobbing in the moonlight.

Dolphin, dolphin now swimming home with glee,
dolphin, dolphin back in the sea.

Dolphin, dolphin, home at last,
captivity, captivity now the past.

Victoria Grout (9)
The Russell School

Red

Red like . . .
The fiery lava
Flowing towards the city
Or the colourful sunset
Shining on the ground.

The dangerous blood-python
That sucks out your blood
Or the loud fireworks
That are in flower shapes.

The burning sun
Bringing light to the earth
Or a dotted ladybird
That flies and eats a leaf.

The dark blood
That flows on the grass
Or a beautiful rose
That grows in the field.

Jasmin Kogelbauer (9)
The Russell School

Red

Red like . . .

A beautiful butterfly
That opens its wings.

The opening rose
Shines in the sun.

A lovely sun
That is in the evening.

Romantic love
Gives happiness to everyone.

A bright heart
That lights up in your body.

Ella Strutt (9)
The Russell School

Orange

As orange as . . .

Fire flames
That spread all around.

Juicy orange
Cut up into pieces.

Yummy peach
That ripens in the fridge.

Sun
Shining in the air.

Trophy
Shiny and metal.

Satsuma
Yummy and squishy.

Clementines
Small and round.

Sunset
Setting down.

Orange juice
Drink it with a straw.

Jessica Tolmia (9)
The Russell School

Red

Red like . . .
A blazing fire that takes down a building
Or a beautiful rose.

Red like . . .
A droplet of blood from a dagger
Or a comet zooming through space.

Red like . . .
A blood python slithering through the grass
Or grapefruit juice that is too sour to drink.

Red like . . .
A shiny stop sign that glitters in the night
Or a ladybird flying in the sky.

Owain Strassburg (8)
The Russell School

Orange

Orange like . . .
A fire that is so hot it can burn your hand off
Or orange juice sitting in a cup

Orange like . . .
A rotten peach that has been left in the fridge for weeks
Or a golden sun shining in the sky

Orange like . . .
A pool of lava that is nearly as hot as the sun
Or a sunflower swaying in the breeze

Orange like . . .
Rotten cheese that has got lots of mould
Or a yummy satsuma that is ripe enough to eat

Orange like . . .
A bucket of tiny old maggots
Or a trophy that is waiting to be won

Orange like . . .
A squished orange that lots of people have stamped on
Or a delicious creamy peach, smooth against your skin.

Amber Grant (9)
The Russell School

Green

Green like . . .

a wet frog diving in a pond
or a hungry grass snake, waiting for its prey.

A big bunch of grapes sitting in a bowl
or a spiky crocodile gobbling up an antelope.

A living leaf
or a tall stinging nettle.

A belly of a basking shark
or a bowl of mushy peas.

Gabriel Alveteg (9)
The Russell School

Green

Green like a crocodile waiting for its kill.
Green like a poisonous snake that slithers along the ground.
Green like a leaf falling from a tree during a storm.
Green like the fresh spring grass after the rain.
Green like a plant growing, reaching towards the sky.

Timur Aydin (8)
The Russell School

Smuggler's Night

Down the dark, shadowy street,
No noise can be heard
Other than my horses' feet
And a tiny bird.

Brandy in one hand,
Baccy in the other
I shuffle along in the thin sand,
Thinking thoughts of my old mother.

Sunrise is it now
I gallop away to the east,
I hear the grunting of a sow,
Thinking thoughts of a feast.

Eleanor Cook (9)
The Russell School

The Smuggler's Night

Down the street
You can hear the horses' feet.
The smugglers silently creeping
While everyone's sleeping.

Smuggling whiskey, brandy and wine
For the ladies', clothes so fine.
Tabacco, chocolate and coffee too
Everything you need comes through.

If you hear a midnight sound
Don't look out, just turn around
Just remember what I said,
Now it's time to go to bed.

Gus Lambri (10)
The Russell School

My Journey To School

This morning, as I was on my way to school,
The world outside started behaving badly.
The trees waved their arms wildly for attention,
While prickly bushes bullied the undergrowth.

Coughing and spluttering the car pushed into the traffic jam,
While the lorries belched and wheezed in the chilling air.
A van, eating its breakfast, filling up for the journey ahead,
While buses sneezed their doors open.

Umbrellas were fighting the rain, keeping people dry
And the wind was spinning the roundabouts.
As things started to quieten down,
We started to line up!

Joshua Archbold (11)
The Russell School

The Giraffe Chorus

King and Queen of the giraffe are we;
No other giraffe so tall we see!
None but we have necks so long!
Eating the leaves all day long!
Munskin, munskin, giraffe jee,
We think no giraffe so happy as we!
Munskin, munskin, giraffe jill,
We think so then, and we thought so still!

Caroline Cooper (10)
The Russell School

My Journey To School

This morning, as I was on my way to school,
The world outside started behaving badly.
The houses, locked out the outside world, stared in sorrow,
Waking from their long night,
The trees rustled and yawned,
As if they were bored.
Our car started up, coughing and spluttering,
The wind whistling and wailing,
Sprinted past buildings, late for work.
With its doors sneezing open,
The school bus trampled off,
The fence around the school was guarding it like soldiers.
When I arrived at school the bell started shrieking!

Florence Kipps (10)
The Russell School

The Monkey Chorus

Lord and Lady of Monkeys are we;
No other chimps so grand we see!
None but we have curling tails!
We're so much faster than those snails!
Cheeky, funny chimps jee,
We think no monkeys so cheeky as we!
Furry silly monkeys are we,
Cunning and clever I'll think you'll agree!

Christopher Hursey (9)
The Russell School

Undercover On A Midnight Mare

Down the shadowy, sleeping street,
You hear the sound of a horse's feet.
Trotting past and clopping by,
Here she comes, so dark, so sly.

A smuggler bringing goods to hide,
Undercover from far and wide.
Creeping here and sneaking there,
Undercover on a midnight mare.

In disguise, so sly and cunning,
Trotting quickly but never running.
When the soldiers come riding through,
Down to the gutter she jumps, it's true.

Crawling in the damp street gutter,
Above a raven's wings do flutter.
Keep hiding smuggler, don't let him see,
Otherwise you won't be free.

Sarah Edwards (10)
The Russell School

Tiger's Eyes

Mine is the eyes that shine no more,
Mine is the heart that will beat no more,
Mine is the legs that will leap no more,
Mine is, mine is,
Mine is the voice that will roar and roar,
Mine is the spirit that will never sleep,
Mine is the body in this cage, and I'm dying
Day by day!

Tiya-Reneé Middleton (11)
The Russell School

Lament Of A Giant Panda

Once I sang with the bamboo sticks
And danced with the trees
I shared my secrets with the birds
And they shared theirs with me.

Now there are no more bamboo sticks
The forest is all sad
For poachers came and killed my friends
And destroyed all we had.

They cut down all the trees in sight
And left the forest bare
The leaves and twigs lay on the floor
Crying in despair.

The corpses were taken far away
And I was left alone
I had no more trees to dance with
In my destroyed home.

Today I'll run far, far away
Never to return
I'll follow the stars to a new land
And back, I will not turn.

Josie Russell (11)
The Russell School

The Naughty World

This morning, as I was on my way to school,
The world outside started behaving badly.
The flowers hip-hopped with the wind, enjoying the amusement,
While the leaves were murmuring about each other.
The sun and the clouds in a game of hide-and-seek played,
And the houses smoked, thinking no one was looking.
The post box, munching letters for breakfast, smiling for more,
Whilst cars were having a loud argument.
The bus stop was bored, it had nothing to do,
Then a bus sneezed his doors open.
The clouds started rolling together.
Finally we reached school and the sky started crying.

Poppy Cawley (11)
The Russell School

My Journey To School

This morning, as I was on my way to school,
The world outside started behaving badly.
The sun started smiling at me,
Scooters were speedily racing down the street.
Bikes pushing people away, 'How rude!'
Rubbish angrily running around.
Vans shouting wildly.
Bus stops waiting patiently,
And when I finally got dropped at school,
The bell rang!

Dominic O'Brien (10)
The Russell School

When I Was Walking To School

This morning, when I was walking to school,
The world started behaving badly.
Trees were dropping litter everywhere,
Like careless teenagers.
Bending over, the flowers seemed to wave,
Just like my brother.
Hedges wailed as they were being cut.
Bicycles were stealing through the streets like burglars.
When I arrived at school
The world had calmed down and nature went to sleep.

Alexander Bustos (11)
The Russell School

Walking To School

This morning, as I was on my way to school,
The world outside started behaving badly.
The sun awoke from its magical sleep in Heaven.
The trees were dancing like ballerinas in a show.
The birds were talking and chattering to one another.
The leaves were doing the foxtrot as they fell to the floor.
Cars, vans and motorbikes were running a marathon
As they vroomed down the road.
As I came to school a robin danced a jig,
By hopping from one leg to the other,
Wishing me a happy day.

Bramble Wallace (11)
The Russell School